Contents

HOMEWORK CLUB

KU-536-874

What happened at Hiroshima?

A shadow over the world – the mushroom cloud created by the Hiroshima bomb.

An unsuspecting city

6 August, 1945 was a fine summer's day. World War II had come to an end in Europe, but still Japanese cities were being heavily bombed. As people tried to work on as normal, little did they realize that for thousands of them life was about to come to a terrifying and violent end. Hiroshima had been selected by the USA as the first atomic bomb target.

Just before 9 am, an American bomber, the *Enola Gay*, appeared over the port of Hiroshima. It was carrying a single atomic bomb weighing over 4500 kg. Although many tests had been done, nobody knew for certain what the effect of dropping an atomic bomb on a major city would be.

Death from the sky

The co-pilot Colonel Paul Tibbets released the bomb and the *Enola Gay* quickly climbed to safety. Less than a minute later the bomb exploded. One eyewitness saw a flash so bright she thought a fire had started in her eyes.

She then realized the skin on her face, hands and arms had peeled off. Although they could not see the devastation through the huge cloud of smoke and dust, one of the *Enola Gay*'s crew cried out, *'My God, what have we done?'* The explosion produced a ground temperature of 3000°C – twice as high as the melting-point of iron. An estimated 50,000 people living within 1 km of the blast burned to death. A wind tore through the city at 800 kph, uprooting trees and flattening buildings.

Survivors staggered around in a state of shock. The dead and dying lay all around. Neighbours and total strangers tried to help each other. But there was chaos everywhere. This city of 245,000 people only had 150 doctors. Of these, 65 were killed outright and most of the rest were wounded. Of 1780 nurses, 1654 were dead or too injured to work. At the city's biggest hospital only one doctor out of thirty was uninjured and only five more were able to work. The nursing staff of over 200 was down to ten. 10,000 wounded poured in desperately seeking help.

Hiroshima was a medium-sized port and industrial centre backed by a ring of mountains which enclosed the force of the blast.

The final toll

No one knows exactly how many died in Hiroshima on 6 August, 1945. Official figures estimated 100,000. As the months went by the figure rose steadily. **Radiation** sickness was taking its toll. By the end of 1945, the estimate was 140,000.

DEATH MARCH

On 7 August, 1945, the day after the bomb was dropped, a Japanese doctor wrote in his diary: *'Hundreds of injured people trying to escape passed our house. Their hands and faces were burned and swollen; great sheets of skin had peeled away like rags on a scarecrow. By this morning there were so many of them lying on both sides of the road it was impossible to pass without stepping on them.'*

How the atom bomb changed the world

The first successful atom bomb test had taken place in July 1945. Robert J Oppenheimer, whose team of scientists made the bomb, said afterwards 'We knew the world would not be the same.' Other people agreed.

On 2 September, 1945, less than a month after atom bombs were dropped on Japan, Douglas MacArthur, an American General, warned that a future war could destroy the entire human race. The terrifying power of atomic weapons made military leaders realize that any country thinking about using one might easily bring disaster on itself as well as its enemy. American General Omar Bradley concluded that *'The way to win an atomic war is to make certain it never starts.'*

Devastated Hiroshima

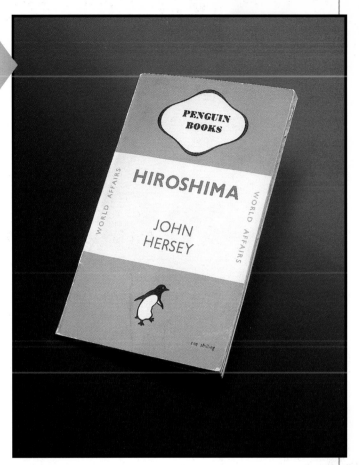

Telling the world

In May 1946, the *New Yorker* magazine sent journalist John Hersey to Japan to find survivors of the attack on Hiroshima. He interviewed two doctors, two priests and two women and wrote about what they had suffered and seen. The *New Yorker's* editor was shocked by Hersey's 30,000 word report. He believed that most people still did not understand how terrible the effects of an atom bomb were.

THE VALUE OF FEAR

In November 1945, Albert Einstein, the world's most famous scientist, wrote:
*'I do not believe that civilization will be wiped out in a war fought with the atomic bomb. Perhaps two thirds of the people of the earth might be killed, but enough men capable of thinking, and enough books, would be left to start again, and civilization could be restored. Since I do not foresee that atomic energy is to be a great **boon** for a long time, I have to say that for the present it is a menace. Perhaps it is as well that it should be. It may **intimidate** the human race into bringing order into its international affairs, which, without the pressure of fear, it would not do.'*

He published Hersey's complete account, using one whole issue of the magazine. He thought this would have more impact than spreading it over several weekly issues. He was right. It sold out within hours. Fifty American newspapers reprinted it. It was broadcast on radio in both America and Britain. America's Book of the Month Club published it as a special 'Extra'. In Britain, Penguin Books published 250,000 paperback copies of it.

The background: how Japan became a threat

Opening up the closed country

In 1639, after many years of civil war, Japan cut off trade with other countries, fearing outsiders might cause yet more problems. In 1853, a modern American fleet demanded the right to trade. Japan had fallen far behind in technology and was forced to agree. This humiliation caused years of crisis and confusion, but by 1873 a new government was in power and was determined to make Japan strong by adopting western-style technology. It used foreign experts and imports to rapidly modernize the armed forces, build railways and set up cotton-mills and steel-works. Western-style banks, schools, coinage, weights and measures, newspapers and postal services were introduced.

Japan's modernized army in action.

Empire building

Japan's leaders compared their country to Britain, a small off-shore island. By conquering a huge overseas empire, Britain had become the most powerful country in the world. Japan wanted to do the same. In 1894, Japan and China fought for control over their neighbour, Korea.

This map shows the growth of the Japanese overseas empire.

On the map:
MANCHURIA (Japanese occupation 1931–2)
MANCHUKUO (1934 Empire under Japanese protection)
JAPAN
KOREA
•Tokyo
•Hiroshima
Nagasaki•
•Shanghai
CHINA
FORMOSA

Japanese Empire before 1928
Occupied by Japan 1928–36

Despite its huge population, China was easily defeated by Japan's more modern armed forces. Japan not only took control of Korea, but also took the Chinese island of Taiwan as the first **colony** of its overseas empire. In 1904–5, Japan fought Russia for control of Korea, and won. In 1910, Korea became part of the Japanese Empire. These successes made Japan's military leaders a powerful influence in government.

TOKYO TRANSFORMED

American teacher W E Griffis was shocked by how poor Japan was when he arrived in rural Echizen in 1870. Within a year he'd been transferred to the capital and was amazed by how it had changed in such a short time:

'Tokyo is so modernized that I scarcely recognize it. There are no beggars on the streets. The age of pantaloons (trousers) has come. Carriages are numerous. The soldiers are all in uniform, as are the police. New bridges span the canals. Gold and silver coins are being used as money in circulation …'

Problems at home

Despite dramatic progress in building modern industries, Japan still had many problems. Rapid population growth kept many people in poverty. In 1923, a massive earthquake destroyed the capital, Tokyo, and the port of Yokohama, killing 100,000 people and destroying or damaging 3,000,000 homes. America gave millions of dollars to help Japan recover, but in 1924 banned **immigration** by Japanese people. Many Japanese took this ban as a racist insult.

Crisis and conquest

A greater Japan

During the 1920s, **extremists** became more active in politics and in the Japanese army. They argued that the best way for Japan to become rich and respected, was to make its empire even bigger. This would provide Japanese industry with the raw materials it needed, such as coal, iron, rubber and oil, and poor people could leave Japan and start new lives overseas.

Bullying China

Japanese businesses built railways and mined for minerals in Manchuria, a huge, underpopulated part of northern China. The weak Chinese government even allowed Japanese troops to guard the mines and railways. But between 1929 and 1931, world trade collapsed and millions of people lost their jobs. 3,000,000 were out of work in Japan. The country's leaders desperately wanted to expand. So, in 1931, the Japanese army faked a Chinese attack on a Manchurian railway, then used this as an excuse to take over the whole area. In 1937, Japanese generals invaded the rest of China and in 1940, Japan took over French **colonies** in south-east Asia.

Japanese expansion 1942–45

Extent of Japanese conquest 1942

Japanese front in 1945 at time of surrender

MANCHURIA

KOREA

JAPAN

Hiroshima • • Tokyo

CHINA

INDIA

Pacific Ocean

Philippine Islands

Success in the Pacific

America protested at Japan's actions. The American government tried to stop Japan's expansion by refusing to sell its government oil or steel. But Japan still refused to withdraw from its conquests. Believing war with America was unavoidable, in December 1941, the Japanese airforce made a devastating surprise attack on the US Navy base at Pearl Harbor, Hawaii. For the next six months Japanese forces triumphed everywhere. They took the Philippines from America, and Hong Kong and Singapore from Britain.

The attack on Pearl Harbor.

The tide turns

Then, in June 1942, the Japanese lost four aircraft-carriers in a decisive naval battle off Midway Island in the Pacific. The weakened Japanese navy was now unable to stop American forces from recapturing Pacific islands. By 1944, the US could send bombers against Japan. But bombing Japan was one thing; invading Japan was quite another. American forces were about to discover just how fiercely the Japanese would defend their territory.

The price of victory

In April 1945, US forces landed on the off-shore Japanese island of Okinawa. It took three months to conquer it. 110,000 of its 120,000 Japanese defenders died in the fighting. 34 US ships were sunk, 368 damaged, 12,500 men killed and 36,600 wounded. If that was the price to be paid for taking one island of 500 square miles what would it cost to take Japan itself?

Origins of the atom bomb

Atoms all around

Everything is made up of atoms – including you. In solid things, like you, the atoms are packed close together. In liquids and gases they move about more. Atoms are incredibly small – the full stop at the end of this sentence has 250,000,000,000 atoms in it. However, atoms themselves are made up of even smaller pieces.

Albert Einstein, the century's most famous scientist.

Scientists working in different countries – like the New Zealander Ernest Rutherford, the Italian-American Enrico Fermi and the German Albert Einstein – gradually came to understand how atoms are made up. They realized it might be possible to build a device which could make these smaller particles crash into each other in a massive series of mini-collisions which would release huge amounts of energy.

If these could be controlled they could produce power for industry – or an immensely powerful explosion. By the 1930s, scientists in most leading industrial countries were aware that it might be possible to create an 'atomic bomb'. Whichever country succeeded in doing so would control a weapon more destructive than any previously invented.

A single neutron splits an atom releasing energy and more neutrons which creates a chain reaction

LETTER TO THE PRESIDENT

On 2 August, 1939, just one month before the outbreak of World War II in Europe, Albert Einstein wrote to US President Franklin D Roosevelt to warn him how recent scientific research could revolutionize warfare:

'Some recent work by E Fermi and L Szilard leads me to expect that the element uranium may be turned into a new and important source of energy in the immediate future. This would also lead to the construction of bombs. A single bomb of this type, carried by boat and exploded in a port, might very well destroy the whole port, together with some of the surrounding territory. However, such bombs might very well prove too heavy for transportation by air.'

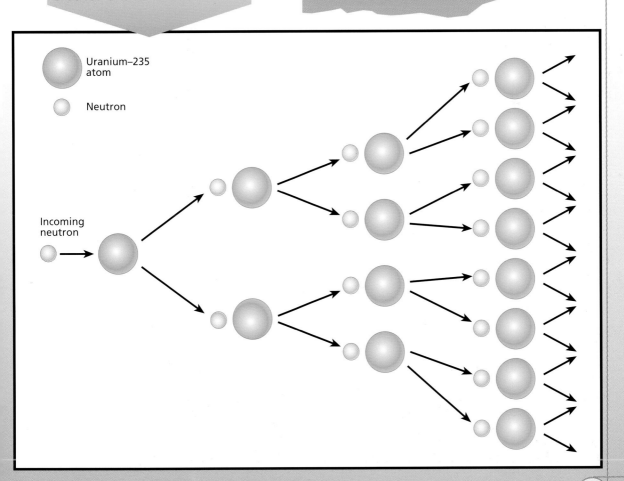

Uranium–235 atom

Neutron

Incoming neutron

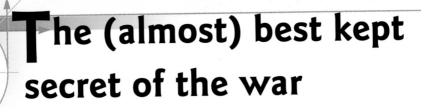

The (almost) best kept secret of the war

The Manhattan Project

The Manhattan Project was the top-secret effort to build an atomic bomb. It took its code name from the district of New York where the early research was done. The scientists working in the USA included Americans, Britons, Canadians and European **refugees**. Their work needed large workshops and laboratories and much special technical equipment. Project centres were also built at remote sites in Tennessee, Washington and New Mexico. The costs involved ran to $2,000,000,000.

The first test

The first atomic bomb was successfully exploded at Alamagordo air base, New Mexico on 16 July, 1945. Placed on a steel tower it created an explosion equal to 20,000 tonnes of TNT. The heat was so intense that the tower simply disappeared and the desert sand 700 metres around its site was turned to glass.

Top secret?...

Only the most important **Allied** leaders and generals knew that there was a bomb project.

'Little Boy' – the bomb that wiped out a city.

Not quite

Thanks to German-born Klaus Fuchs, who worked on the Manhattan Project but was also a Soviet agent, Stalin, leader of the **USSR**, also knew about the bomb project.

In fact the war in Europe had ended when the first bomb was exploded. But thousands of men were being transported to the Far East, to prepare for the invasion of Japan. The war there was expected to last at least another year and a half. Even Allied commanders in the area had no idea that it would be over within a month.

Japanese efforts to make an atomic bomb had been held back by shortages of staff and money. The scientists themselves did not think the matter urgent because they believed that, although in theory it was possible to make one, in practice, not even the USA would be able to do so in the foreseeable future. German scientists were also working on a bomb project but had to give up when Norwegian resistance fighters **sabotaged** the underground factory making material they needed.

Robert J. Oppenheimer and General Groves examine the remains of the steel tower which had supported the first A-bomb successfully exploded

A JAPANESE BOMB?

In 1949, researcher Chitoshi Yanaga admitted that, when news about Hiroshima leaked through to them *Japanese scientists knew immediately that it was the atomic bomb, for they too had been working on it for years.'* In the two weeks between Japan's surrender and the arrival of US occupation forces much of the evidence of this work was deliberately destroyed.

No alternative?

Raids fail to break Japan

In March 1945, 300 American bombers launched a massive night raid on Tokyo, the Japanese capital. In just two hours 89,000 people were killed and 130,000 more were injured. Many burned alive, others choked for lack of oxygen, others drowned seeking safety in the Tsumida river. Over the next week the big industrial cities of Nagoya, Osaka and Kobe were similarly attacked. But still Japan fought on.

Unconditional surrender

In May 1945, Germany surrendered to the **Allies**. The leaders of the US, **USSR** and Great Britain met at Potsdam in Germany to agree the terms of peace in Europe. They called on Japan to surrender without any conditions, giving up all its overseas territories. The only promise the Allies made was that the Japanese would not be enslaved, nor their country destroyed if they surrendered. Experts on Japan advised the Allied leaders that ordinary Japanese people would obey their government despite hardship and that an invasion would cost many lives.

The Potsdam meeting, July 1945. Attlee of Britain, Truman of America and Stalin of the USSR.

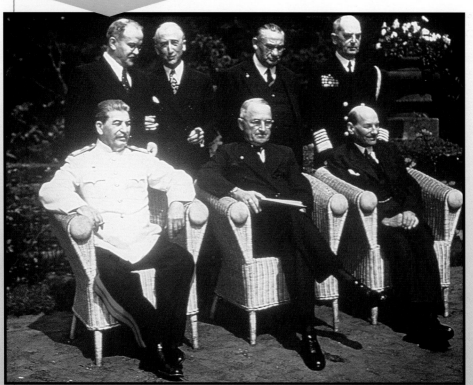

The decision to drop the atomic bomb

US President Truman claimed that he never had any doubts about using the atom bomb to speed the end of the war and avoid a bloody invasion.

Some historians have suggested that he also wanted to demonstrate the bomb's immense power to the USSR. America and the USSR had never been comfortable as allies because America wanted to hold back the spread of **communism**.

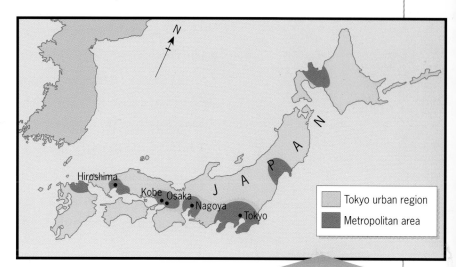

The big industrial cities of Japan in 1945.

Others ask why the Allies did not explode an atomic bomb off-shore as a warning. This would have given Japan another chance to surrender before the bomb was actually used on a city. But perhaps the scientists were not 100 per cent sure it would really work.

DROPPING THE BOMB

Professor Leo Szilard, Manhattan Project:

'*We scientists thought we were in a neck-and-neck race with the Germans and that getting the bomb first might mean the difference between winning and losing the war. But, when Germany was defeated, many of us became uneasy about the proposed use of the bomb in the war with Japan.*'

US Admiral Leahy: '*The use of this barbarous weapon was of no material assistance. The Japanese were already defeated because of the effective sea blockade and successful bombing.*'

Hisatune Sakomizu, Secretary to the Japanese Cabinet: '*The atomic bomb (A-bomb) sacrificed many people other than Japanese military. This provided us with an excuse to end the war to save innocent Japanese civilians. If the A-bomb had not been dropped we would have had great difficulty in finding a good reason to end the war.*'

Why did Japan surrender?

Soldiering on

On 7 August, 1945, the day after Hiroshima's destruction, Japanese radio simply announced that it had been attacked with 'a new kind of bomb'. No contact was made with the **Allies**. Instead Japan, which was not at war with the **USSR**, tried to persuade the Russians to become a go-between to start **negotiations** for peace. On 8 August, the Japanese ambassador met the Soviet Foreign Minister – who told him the USSR was declaring war on Japan. Two hours later **Soviet** troops invaded Manchuria.

The second bomb

On 9 August, another A-bomb was dropped, on the port of Nagasaki. Although it was much more powerful than the Hiroshima bomb, it did less damage because the city's hilly site lessened the force of the blast. Even so about 50,000 people died and a third of all buildings were completely destroyed.

Some Japanese generals still wanted to fight on. Japan is very mountainous, an ideal country for **guerrilla** fighting. Resistance like the defence of Okinawa could cost an invader perhaps a million casualties. Japanese **extremists** were prepared to fight on, with civilians armed with bamboo spears prepared to suffer high casualties in order to defend Japan and force a negotiated peace.

Nagasaki was a major ship-building centre.

The Japanese government was completely divided over what to do. In the end the Emperor broke the deadlock and Japan surrendered on 14 August, 1945.

Were the bombs decisive?

It seemed obvious to many people that the atom bombs hastened the end of the war and so saved the lives an invasion would have cost. But the war might have been ended in other ways. Ordinary bombing could have continued, without a land invasion, until Japan gave in. Some Japanese leaders feared their rice fields would be fire-bombed just before harvest – the country could have been starved out.

Living in the ashes – a Japanese family camp out in the ruins of their Nagasaki home.

Were the USSR's actions decisive?

Some people argue that the USSR's declaration of war against Japan speeded up Japan's surrender. They suggest that Japanese leaders feared an invasion by both the USSR and the US-led Allies. They thought Japan would be permanently divided between the invaders. This did happen in Germany. Worse still, if the USSR took over all of Japan, it would abolish the Emperor and establish a **communist** government. As the Japanese wanted to keep their old ways of ruling, surrendering quickly to the USA, which was likely to be a less brutal occupier, seemed the best option.

Occupation and reconstructio

A positive partnership

When US troops landed in Japan on 28 August, both sides feared violence. The Americans expected **fanatics** to make sneak attacks on them. The Japanese were afraid their homes would be looted. In fact, the **occupation** turned out better than anyone had dared hope. The Japanese military disarmed obediently. The **Allies** decided not to blame the Emperor for the war but to use his authority to get Japanese co-operation in carrying out important reforms:

• Japan became a **democracy**. All men and women were given the vote and equal legal rights. Free **trade unions** were allowed.

• Land was given to poor farmers. No one was allowed to own big estates.

• School textbooks which had praised war were rewritten. Education was opened up to more people, especially to women.

The commander of Allied occupation forces, General Douglas MacArthur, became very popular with the Japanese. The Emperor went out, in civilian clothes and not military uniform, and met ordinary people face to face for the first time.

The democratic Emperor, Hirohito, dressed in civilian clothes after the war.

Rebuilding from the ashes

By the end of the war Japan had lost 80 per cent of its shipping. A third of all industrial machinery and a quarter of all buildings had been destroyed by bombing. Only the ancient cities of Kyoto, Nara and Kamakura had been spared. If US forces had not brought in emergency food supplies many Japanese would have starved in the first winter after the war. By 1955, Japanese living standards were as high as they had been in 1936. In 1955, Japan manufactured the world's first transistor radio. By 1964, Japan was rich enough to host the Olympics – and make 400,000,000 radios a year.

The new Japan is peaceful and prosperous.

THE BENEFITS OF WAR

American historian John Dower argues that the war boosted Japanese industry: *'In the long view, the Japanese benefited by losing the war. The destruction caused by the air raids actually hastened the construction of more up-to-date factories. Of the eleven major auto manufacturers in postwar Japan, ten came out of the war years. Shipping, cameras, binoculars, watches and the like were similarly grounded in technologies given priority during the war. Sewing machines were produced by factories converted from making machine guns. The number of technical schools increased from eleven to over four hundred between 1935 and 1945.'*

A long time dying

Almost everyone within one kilometre of the centre of the atom bomb explosions died, most instantly, the rest within a week, as a result of burns or internal bleeding from organs damaged by the blast. Anyone who was in either city within 100 hours of the explosion received a dangerous dose of radiation.

After-effects of the atom bomb

Many survivors who were not badly burned, later developed sores, lost their hair or suffered from **cataracts** on their eyes. Severe burn victims were disfigured by hard, swollen scars. Radiation victims were prone to blood diseases and cancers. Sixty babies born to mothers exposed to radiation had abnormally small heads; half of these failed to achieve normal levels of intelligence.

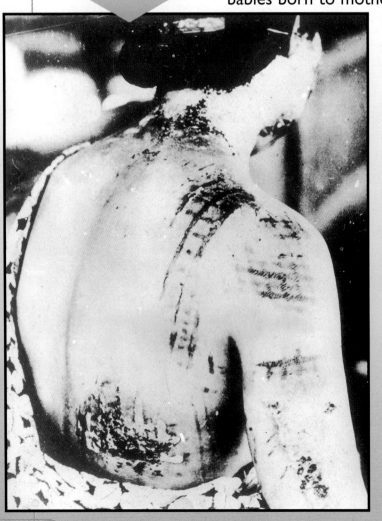

An A-bomb victim with burn scars.

Most atomic bomb survivors – known as *hibakusha* in Japanese – faced a life of poor health and poverty. In 1951, Japan signed a **treaty** with America. The Americans would leave Japan. But in return, Japan had to give up any claim against the USA for compensation for *hibakusha*.

Caring for survivors

Hibakusha formed self-help groups and campaigned for help from the Japanese government. In 1957, the Japanese government finally passed a law giving them free medical care. 360,000 people qualified for it.

In 1968, the government announced special payments for *hibakusha*. But, by 1976, only about a third of them had received some aid. The city governments of Hiroshima and Nagasaki, supported by charities, took the lead in caring for *hibakusha* through special hospitals, nursing homes, orphanages and workshops. Since 1946 both cities have held annual memorial services for victims and supported organizations working for world peace.

SYMBOL OF SURVIVAL

The concrete domed trade centre which survived the Hiroshima explosion became the centre of a Peace Park where a museum was built and peace rallies held. A proposal to demolish the ruined building was angrily rejected by an organization of A-bomb survivors: *'We surviving victims have made a solemn pledge that the same terrible disaster must never be repeated. We should retain the dome as a monument dedicated to peace for all mankind. The atomic bomb is known to all the world, but only for its power. It is still not known what hell the Hiroshima people went through, nor how they continue to suffer from radiation illnesses even today, nineteen years after the bombing.'* In 1966, the Hiroshima city government voted that the building should be permanently preserved.

The Hiroshima Dome was built as a trade exhibition centre. This steel-reinforced concrete structure was right under the centre of the blast.

Balance of fear

Cold War

During World War II the **communist USSR** and the western **democracies** had joined together to fight Nazi Germany. But they supported two different ways of living and could not work together after the war. The USSR helped Communists take over governments throughout eastern Europe. This alarmed western democracies. A 'Cold War' rivalry developed. Each side built up weapons and military alliances. In 1949, the democracies formed the North Atlantic **Treaty** Organization (NATO) under American leadership. That same year the USSR tested its first atomic bomb, showing that both sides now had them. In 1952, America tested the world's first H-(hydrogen) bomb, which was far more powerful than the Hiroshima bomb. By 1953, the USSR also had the H-bomb. In 1955, the USSR founded a communist military alliance, the Warsaw Pact.

The Cuban crisis

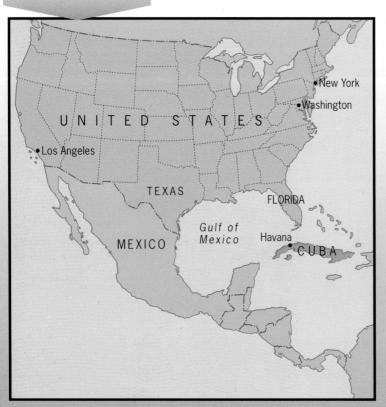

Crisis over Cuba

In October 1962, the world came to the edge of war when the USSR sent ships to pro-communist Cuba to install atomic missiles, targeted on the USA. American President John F. Kennedy ordered the US Navy to prevent the Soviet ships from reaching Cuba.

As the moment of contact approached, Soviet leader, Khrushchev, ordered the ships to turn back rather than risk war. As a result of this crisis a direct 'hot line' was installed between Washington and Moscow, so that US and Soviet leaders could communicate immediately in an emergency. In 1963, the USA, USSR and Britain agreed not to carry out atom bomb tests in the atmosphere, in outer space or under water.

End of an era

The break-up of the USSR between 1985 and 1989 meant the Cold War was over. Russian troops withdrew from eastern Europe and the Warsaw Pact broke up. Former communist countries – Poland, Hungary and the Czech Republic – applied to join NATO. The USA and USSR agreed to reduce their atomic weapons by stages.

Protesting for peace at Greenham Common.

BAN THE BOMB!

In western countries people who thought atomic weapons too terrible to use organized protest movements. Britain's Campaign for Nuclear **Disarmament** (CND), founded in 1958, organized an annual march from the Atomic Weapons Research Establishment at Aldermaston, Berkshire, ending with a rally in London's Trafalgar Square. Between 1981 and 1991, dozens of women camped outside the air force base at Greenham Common, Berkshire, to protest against the presence there of American Cruise missiles with atomic warheads.

Atoms for peace

Pioneering uses

In 1951, Britain opened the world's first centre for treating cancer by using radioactive **cobalt** manufactured in Canada. Over the next 30 years 13,000,000 person-years of life would be saved by this method.

In 1954, the world's first atomic power station, with a capacity of 5000 **kilowatts**, began generating electricity near Moscow. The first large atomic power station, with 90,000 kilowatts capacity, opened at Calder Hall in Britain's Lake District in 1956. By 1990, the USA had over 100 nuclear power plants.

The US Navy realized nuclear power could be used to keep ships sailing for long periods without needing to refuel. In 1954, it launched the world's first atomic-powered submarine *Nautilus*. Its first voyage lasted two years, and covered over 110,000 km. In 1958, *Nautilus* made the first ever journey under the ice cap of the North Pole, crossing the 3000 kilometres in 96 hours.

USS *Nautilus* was the first atomic-powered submarine.

International co-operation

In 1955, an International Conference on the Peaceful Uses of Atomic Energy was held in Switzerland. Scientists from 73 countries were able to meet together for the first time and learn from each other's work.

Nuclear power in Japan

Because Japan is the only nation to have suffered an atomic attack, the Japanese might have been expected to distrust even peaceful uses of atomic power. Many did. But the rapid growth of Japan's industries needed ever more energy. Rising oil prices made government and businesses eager to find alternatives. By 1990, Japan was the world's fourth largest producer of nuclear power – the nation's largest single source of electricity.

MELTDOWN !

In 1979, a serious accident occurred at the atomic power plant at Three Mile Island, Pennsylvania USA. 100,000 local residents had to be moved temporarily because of the danger from escaping gases. It was later shown that workers had not understood what was happening and had turned off safety devices by mistake. The worst nuclear accident to date happened at Chernobyl in the Ukraine in 1986. A reactor exploded during an experiment, killing 31 workers and sending 500 more to hospital. Everyone living within 30 km was **evacuated**. Winds carried radioactive fallout as far away as Wales. Ten years later the area around Chernobyl was still poisoned and local people suffered above-average levels of cancer, **leukemia** and other illnesses caused by radiation. Despite this, two of the original four reactors were still being used.

Price of progress

There is no going backwards with inventions and discoveries, however difficult the problems they produce.

Technology marches on

Since 1945, technology has advanced so far that a single Trident nuclear missile, launched 6400 km away from a submarine deep under water, can hit eight targets over an area of 1500 square km. The Neutron bomb, developed in the 1970s, is small enough to be fired from an artillery gun. It is designed to kill by radiation not blast, so that people in the area affected would die in a matter of days, while buildings would be left intact. But despite many people's fears, no country has yet used their atomic weapons and elaborate safety systems have been developed to prevent them from being fired by accident. Meanwhile great progress has also been made in the use of nuclear technology for peaceful purposes, especially to produce electricity.

An air pollution monitor in central Tokyo.

Environmental risks

Accidents like the disaster at Chernobyl have warned us that nuclear power stations can pollute the air we breathe and the water we drink. Finding safe ways and places to dispose of the waste by-products from nuclear plants has become a difficult issue. Even sealed in concrete drums nuclear waste can still remain dangerous for 10,000 years.

Political threats

The first countries to have atomic weapons – the USA, **USSR**, China, Britain and France – have tried to stop other countries getting them. They say that the fewer countries that have these weapons, the less risk there is of them being used – on purpose or accidentally.

The threat of nuclear waste on the reactor of a decaying submarine.

But other countries want the power nuclear weapons bring. India tested its own bomb in 1974. South Africa, Pakistan, Brazil and Israel probably have the technology to produce their own as well. Iraq has also tried to develop nuclear weapons. Since the break-up of the **Soviet** Union, Russian nuclear forces have become neglected. This increases the risk of accidental pollution from abandoned weapons. Worse still is the chance that a nuclear device might fall into the hands of an **extremist** government or terrorists who were prepared to use them. **Dismantling** unwanted weapons is proving expensive, though the USA is helping to pay for this.

The atom bomb has been called the ultimate weapon. The devastation of Hiroshima was so dreadful that no-one has repeated it. Perhaps it has made military leaders think more carefully about the consequences of their actions. Some people feel that the threat of the bomb's use has kept the peace between the major powers for the last 40 years. Other people think it is a threat hanging over the world and that even peaceful uses of nuclear energy are too risky.

Time-line

1639	Japan cuts off foreign trade
1853	USA forces Japan to re-open foreign trade
1894	Japan defeats China and takes over Taiwan
1905	Japan defeats Russia
1910	Japan takes over Korea
1923	Earthquake destroys Tokyo and Yokohama
1924	USA bans immigration by Japanese
1929	World trade collapses
1931	Japan takes over Manchuria
1937	Japan attempts to conquer all of China
1941	December 7th – Japan attacks US naval base at Pearl Harbor, Hawaii
1942	June – Japanese navy defeated at Battle of Midway
1944	US begins bombing of Japan
1945	March – US bombers devastate Tokyo
	April – US forces invade Okinawa
	May – Germany surrenders
	July 16 – First successful atom bomb test at Alamagordo air base, New Mexico
	August 6 – Atom bomb dropped on Hiroshima
	August 8 – USSR declares war on Japan
	August 9 – Atom bomb dropped on Nagasaki
	August 14 – Japan surrenders
	August 28 – US troops land in Japan
1949	North Atlantic **Treaty** Organization founded
1951	Peace treaty signed between Japan and USA
1952	USA tests first Hydrogen bomb
1954	USS *Nautilus* launched
1955	USSR found the Warsaw pact
1964	Olympic games held in Tokyo
1974	India tests an atomic bomb
1979	Nuclear radiation leak at Three Mile Island, Pennsylvania
1986	Nuclear reactor meltdown at Chernobyl, Ukraine
1991	Break-up of USSR ends Cold War

Glossary

Allies	friendly nations
blockade	use ships to prevent goods entering a country
boon	something that is useful
cataract	a clouding of the lens of the eye, causing loss of sight
cobalt	silver-white metal which can be made radioactive to cure some kinds of cancer
colony	land in one place ruled by a foreign government in another place
communism	system of government based on the idea that a single ruling political party can run a country for all its people's benefit better than if they are left to make their own decisions and keep their own private homes, land and businesses
democracy	system of government based on the idea that all citizens have equal rights to speak on political matters and take part freely in choosing and changing their leaders
disarmament	giving up weapons
dismantle	take to pieces
evacuated	taken to safety
extremist	someone with such strong views that they are not prepared to give way
fanatic	extremist who is prepared to use violence
guerrilla	irregular fighter, not part of a recognised army
immigration	people going to live in one country from another country
intimidate	frighten
kilowatts	thousand watts; a watt is the basic unit for measuring electricity
leukemia	a cancer of the blood
negotiations	settle a problem or dispute by talking; usually both sides agree to give up part of their demands
occupation	rule by a foreign army
radiation	energy given off by atomic material
refugees	people forced to leave their home or country
sabotage	deliberate damage to stop something working properly
Soviet	belonging to the Soviet Union (USSR)
trade union	organization to protect and improve the rights and interests of workers
treaty	official agreement between different countries
USSR	Union of Soviet Socialist Republics; an empire in which communist Russia controlled neighbouring countries from 1917 to 1991

Index